Contents

All About Me

My name is Henna Parekh and I am eight years old. I am a *Hindu* and I live in Preston, in Lancashire.

Lots of Hindus live in Preston. Some of us have moved here from India, and some were born here, like me.

Hindu
Community

Kate Taylor and Henna Parekh

Photography by Chris Fairclough

W
FRANKLIN WATTS
LONDON•SYDNEY

This edition 2007
©2005 Franklin Watts

First published in 2005 by
Franklin Watts
338 Euston Road
London NW1 3BH

Franklin Watts Australia
Level 17/207 Kent Street
Sydney, NSW 2000

ISBN: 978 0 7496 7369 7

A CIP catalogue record for this book
is available from the British Library

Printed in Malaysia
Planning and production by Discovery Books Limited
Editor: Laura Durman
Designer: Ian Winton

The author, packager and publisher would like to
thank the following people for their participation in
this book:
    The Parekh family
    The Gujarat Hindu Society
    Priscilla Dhabi
    Molly Smith
    St Andrew's C. of E. School
    Discount Auto Spares

Franklin Watts is a division of Hachette Children's
Books.

I live in this house with my eleven-year-old brother, Niraj, mum, dad and nana.

Me and Niraj have our own bedrooms. My nana sometimes shares mine if we have people to stay. My bedroom is pink. Niraj has football posters all over his bedroom walls.

My Family

**Most of my family live in Preston.
I have relatives in India too.**

My dad, Kamal (on the right), is from Gujarat in India. He goes back sometimes to visit his family. I have been with him twice.

My nana, Savita, is from India too. She came to England in 1967 with my mum and her brothers.

My mum, Anju, was born in Kenya, in Africa. She moved to Preston when she was five years old and her brothers all live nearby.

Me with my mum. ▶

◀ **Me with my cousin, Vandana.**

Where I Live

I like where I live. Lots of my
friends and family live nearby.

On my street, people are always chatting to each other.
We get on well with all of our neighbours.

There is a big park around the corner where I go with Niraj. Our cousins usually come and play with us. I like going on the swings.

▼ **Niraj with our cousins.**

There are lots of nice places to walk. I love walking by the canal.

Markets and Shops

There are lots of different shops where I live, and a busy market too.

Mum does most of our shopping in a big supermarket, but on Sundays she takes me to a good market in town. It's really fun there and sometimes I buy things like earrings or necklaces.

The market. ▶

My dad takes his car to the local mechanic. He is called Anil Chohan. I often go into the garage shop. The people are really friendly and speak to me in *Gujarati*.

◀ **At the local garage shop.**

These pictures show the inside and outside of my dad's shop. He makes and sells lots of different Indian foods, like *samosas*, *chapattis* and *curries*.

My School

**I go to a school called St Andrew's.
I like all of my teachers.**

My favourite subject is English because I enjoy
reading and writing. My worst subject is
maths. I wish I didn't have to do it!

▲ **This is my class.**

At breaktime I play outside with my friends, unless it's raining.

Friday is my best day at school. We have chips for lunch and I go swimming, which is great.

Sometimes we get to do fun experiments in my science class, too.

◄ **In my science class.**

My Friends

I have lots of friends at school and in my community, but I have two best friends.

Molly is my best friend at school. She comes and plays at my house sometimes, but she lives on the other side of Preston.

▶ **Me and Molly in the park.**

My best friend outside school is Priscilla. She's a Hindu like me and lives on our road. Sometimes her mum teaches us Indian dancing, which I love.

▼ **My friend Priscilla.**

14

For my birthday party, all of my friends came over. It was really amazing. My mum made us sandwiches, samosas and *onion bhajis*.

TO WISH YOU A
Happy Birthday

Happy Birthday

To Henna,

Happy birthday

Have a fun birthday!

Love from
Sunita
X X X

Food

I am a *vegetarian*. I love Indian
food but I also like pasta and pizza.

All my family are vegetarians,
and we usually eat Indian
food at home. My dad can
make 98 different kinds
of vegetable curry.

My favourite food is paneer. It's a type of Indian cheese made from *curd*.

For dessert I like chocolate barfi, which is like fudge with chocolate on top. I also like kaju katri, which is made from cashew nuts and is shaped like a diamond.

▶ **Chocolate barfi, yum!**

My Hobbies

My two main hobbies are going to *Brownies* and learning Indian dance.

I go to Brownies every Monday after school for an hour.

I've got loads of friends there. We do lots of different things but my favourite is when we go camping. This year we're going to cook our meals around a fire. I can't wait!

◀ **My *Brown Owl* always meets me at the door.**

I've just started going to Indian dance classes
at the temple. My teacher, Swati, is really nice.
I also want to learn *Bollywood* dancing.
It's really pretty to watch.

◀ **Me dancing
with my mum.**

Languages

I speak two languages: Gujarati, which is an Indian language, and English.

On Saturday mornings I go to Gujarati classes at the temple with Niraj.

We learn the alphabet and how to read, write and speak Gujarati.

▶ **Me and a friend in my Gujarati class.**

◀ **My Gujarati exercise book.**

20

My nana doesn't speak English so I have to speak Gujarati to her. Sometimes I make mistakes and end up saying the wrong thing. It's funny.

I have a book written in Gujarati and English. I read to my nana in English and she reads to me in Gujarati. That way we both learn.

Clothes

I have lots of pretty Indian clothes called *Punjabi suits*. When I'm at home though, I usually wear jeans and jumpers.

My favourite Punjabi suit is pink. Children wear Punjabi suits, but when I'm older I'll wear a *sari* like my mum.

▶ **Me showing Molly my favourite Punjabi suit.**

I have lots of different coloured bracelets to wear with my outfits.

My mum only wears her sari for special occasions but my nana wears one all the time.

Niraj sometimes wears an outfit called a kurta pyjama, which is a long top and trousers.

Music

I listen to all sorts of music. I like English pop songs and music from India.

My favourite songs are from Bollywood films.
Niraj listens to R&B, hip-hop and *Bhangra* music.

My favourite Bollywood CD. ▶

Playing music at the temple. ▶

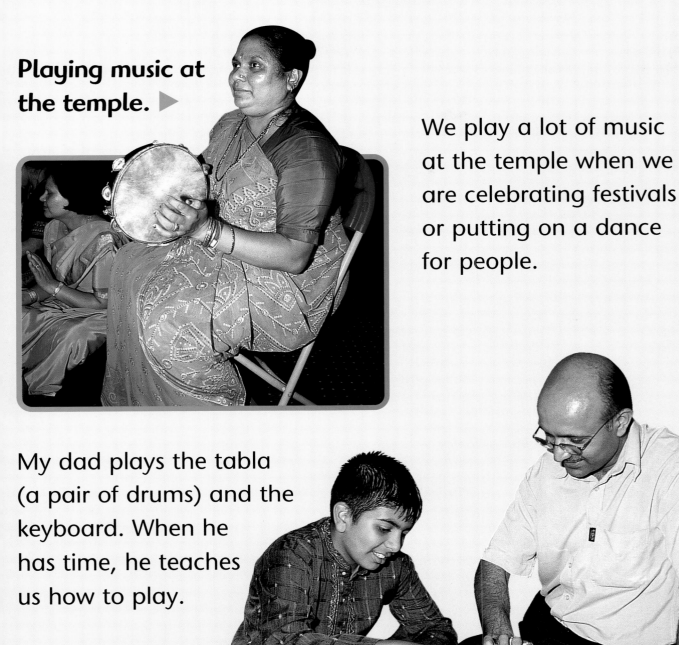

We play a lot of music at the temple when we are celebrating festivals or putting on a dance for people.

My dad plays the tabla (a pair of drums) and the keyboard. When he has time, he teaches us how to play.

▼ **Tabla drums.**

PAUL &CO

25

Religion

My family follows a religion called Hinduism. I pray every day.

There are lots of deities (gods and goddesses) in the Hindu religion. Every morning I go into the prayer room in my house and pray in front of the altar.

On our altar we have images of Krishna and Radha, our favourite deities.

On Sunday mornings I go to the temple with my family to pray and sing bhajans (religious songs).

Whenever I enter the temple, I have to ring a bell so the gods know I'm there.

Festivals

We celebrate lots of festivals all through the year. My favourite one is called Navaratri.

Holi is a really fun festival that we celebrate in Spring. We run around the car park outside the temple throwing coloured powder, called gulal, at each other.

Navaratri takes place in September or October. I go to the temple every day for nine days to celebrate. We sing special songs called garbas and bang sticks together in a religious dance called Dandia Ras.

Diwali, the festival of lights, takes place in October or November.

We decorate our homes with candles and lights and draw patterns, called rangolis, on the ground outside with coloured powder.

My Future

I like living in Preston. I have lots of friends and most of my family live here too. I like going to India but I think I'll stay in Preston when I'm older.

Glossary

Bhangra A popular style of Punjabi music.

Bollywood The Indian film industry, often producing colourful and lively musicals with a special style of dancing, singing and acting.

Brown Owl The adult leader of a Brownies club.

Brownies A club for girls aged between 7 and 10. Part of the Guides Association.

Chapatti A thin Indian bread.

Curd A thickened form of milk, often used to make cheese.

Curry An Indian dish of meat or vegetables flavoured with spices and usually eaten with rice.

Gujarati An Indian language from the state of Gujarat.

Hindu A person who believes in an Indian religion called Hinduism.

Onion bhajis A small flat cake or ball made of vegetables, onion and spices fried in oil.

Punjabi suit A tunic and a pair of trousers, often decorated with sequins and coloured patterns.

Samosa An Indian snack shaped like a triangle and filled with spicy vegetables or meat.

Sari An item of clothing made from a long piece of material that is wrapped around the body.

Vegetarian A person who does not eat any meat.

Index